That's BINGZY!

Let's Talk About It
Discuss & Do Activities

BUILDING SELF-ESTEEM • BUILDING CHARACTER

Written by

Arlene Richards and Mary Taylor

Illustrated by Melissa Martin

Contributions by Grace Busby, Valeria McCray,
Angela Vinez, and Lisa Love

Edited by Indigo Editing & Publications

For more information or ordering, please address:
Bing Note, Inc.
Post Office Box 3645
Oakland, CA 94609
www.bingnote.com

Table of Contents

Welcome to That's Bingzy! Discuss & Do Activity Book

Young children ages three to seven will enjoy these fun activities while engaged in meaningful conversations about life-affirming concepts called Builder-Uppers. These include: I Am Strong, Powerful, Healthy, Loving, Harmonious, Creative, Successful, and Happy. Suited for counselors, teachers, parents, and child care providers, these activities are a tool for both individual or small group interaction.

Bingzy, a bee-like little fellow, is the main character and guide of this book. Bingzy is based on Arlene Richards' book, *That's Bingzy! Busy Building Self-Esteem.*

Guidelines for the Discuss & Do Activity Book

1. Describe Bingzy as the children's little friend who sends them happy thoughts through poems and fun activities.
2. Become familiar with the questions preceding each of the eight sections (six worksheets per section). The questions are to promote more interaction as you guide the children through the Builder-Uppers.
3. The worksheets are to stimulate conversation and develop language to express the major Builder-Upper concepts. To be most effective, adequate discussion time should be devoted to each page.
4. Allow the children to express themselves openly, without the fear of being corrected as right or wrong. Bingzy is there to help them see themselves in a more positive light. Therefore, a nonjudgmental atmosphere is vital.
5. Readers should read the text. Nonreaders can repeat the text after the leader to become acquainted with the vocabulary. (Older students may choose to memorize a poem or two.)
6. Encourage the children to share what Bingzy teaches with their parents, siblings, and friends. This will help to reinforce the positive concepts they learn.
7. Show enthusiasm for the activities and refer to Bingzy and the Builder-Uppers during the day.
8. Lead the children in seeing themselves as valuable individuals who can do many things, even as young children.

Be sure to check out supplemental items that can add enrichment to the Discuss & Do Activity Book at www.bingnote.com:

- ★ *That's Bingzy! Busy Building Self-Esteem* picture book and CD
- ★ Bingzy hand puppet
- ★ Bingzy's Builder-Uppers poster

Bingzy's Builder-Uppers

I AM STRONG
AND POWERFUL,
HEALTHY AND LOVING,
HARMONIOUS
AND CREATIVE,
SUCCESSFUL
AND HAPPY...
AND I LIKE ME!

Builder-Upper:
I Am Strong!

Bingzy says, "Keep trying and never give up."

I Am Strong: I do not give up.

Read the questions and discuss.

1. What does it mean to not give up?
2. When did you show you were strong by completing your homework?
3. How can you be strong during an emergency?
4. During a game, what can you say to encourage a friend who is about to give up?
5. What words are encouraging words?
6. What did someone say to encourage you?

Name: ______________________________

Builder-Upper:
I Am Strong!

Bingzy says, "Being strong means I should keep trying."

Read aloud and discuss.

We lost the game, Bingzy.
We didn't get a hit.
I'm so sad and angry,
I think I'll just quit!

Oh no, little buddy.
You're better than that.
No one wins every time
They go to bat.

Tell the team not to give up,
But to work hard and try to win.
Believe in yourself and each other.
Soon you'll score again.

READ & DISCUSS

What does it mean to get discouraged?

Have you ever felt like you wanted to give up and just quit?

Talk with someone about those feelings.

Name: ____________________

Builder-Upper:
I Am Strong!

Bingzy says, "Be strong and finish your homework, even when friends beg you to come out and play."

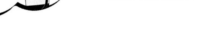

Read aloud and discuss.

"Come out and play," begged Mike today.
What a big problem. What should I say?
I have homework and won't get through
If I stop to play a game with you.

Play before homework is against Mom's rule.
Tomorrow I'll be sad when I get to school.
My teacher will frown and then she'll exclaim,
"You have a fat zero right next to your name!"

READ & DISCUSS

Should I always obey Mom's rules? Why?

How can I find time to play with friends?

How does homework help me in school?

Name: ______________________________

Builder-Upper:
I Am Strong!

Bingzy says, "Being strong is doing your best with what you have and never giving up."

READ & DISCUSS

Bingzy's friend, Jake, has a physical challenge. He shows he is strong by never giving up.

How do you think Jake wants to be treated?

If you were Jake, how would you want to be treated?

Why do you think Bingzy and Jake are good friends?

Do you know anyone who has special challenges? They can make very good friends.

Name: ______________________________

Builder-Upper:
I Am Strong!

Bingzy says, "Strength comes from inside."

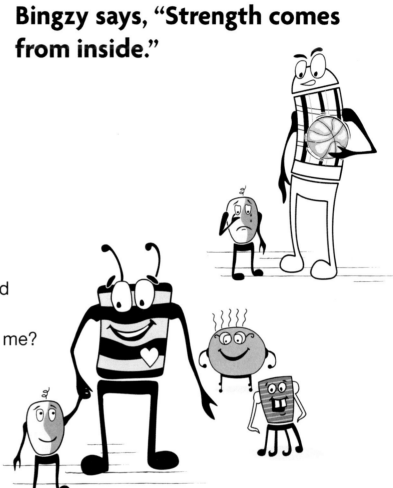

Read aloud and discuss.

I'm not as tall as my brother
And I'm not as fast as Dan.
I can't run or jump or do anything
As well as Dan can.

Sometimes I cry and get really mad
And he calls me a baby.
I wonder, will he ever stop teasing me?
Yes, no, or maybe?

Bingzy says I can be strong,
That strength comes from inside.
He says to just be myself
And never run and hide.

Bingzy says that I am special
And that I can lead someday.
By learning to be strong inside,
Good things will come my way.

READ & DISCUSS

Does anyone tease or bully you, and make you feel bad about yourself? What do you think it means to be strong? Have you treated someone unfairly?

Talk to your parents or teacher. Ask them what you should do when someone treats you unfairly or is rough with you.

Name: ______________________________

Builder-Upper:
I Am Strong!

Bingzy says, "There are some things everyone needs to know in case of an emergency. Being prepared is another way to take care of yourself and be strong."

You should know:

Your full name (not nickname)

____

Your age

____

Your address

____

Your mother's name

____

Your father's name

____

Your home telephone number

____

ACTIVITY **Circle Yes or No**

1. **Should you give this information to a police officer if you are lost?**
   Yes No
2. **Should you give this information to a doctor or nurse if you are hurt?**
   Yes No
3. **Should you give this information to a stranger?**
   Yes No

Ask your parents who you should give this kind of information to, and who you should not.

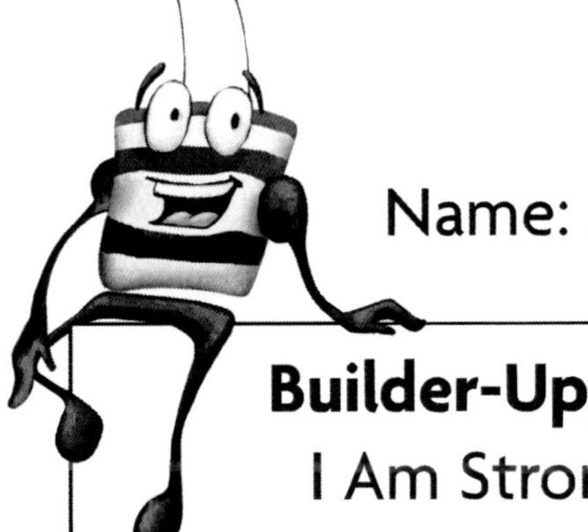

Name: ____________________

Builder-Upper:
I Am Strong!

Bingzy says, "Being strong is being prepared for whatever happens."

READ & DISCUSS

Does your family have a special place to meet during an emergency?

Does your family have an emergency kit?
If they don't, talk to your parents and see if they will start to build one this weekend. If they already have a kit, ask to see it. Become familiar with its contents and where it is kept.

Your family emergency kit could be kept in a plastic trash can on rollers or wherever it is most convenient. You may want to include the following items, but you can adjust it to fit your own family's needs.

Water
Food that won't spoil
Radio (batteries or solar)
Can opener
Emergency telephone numbers
Toothpaste, toothbrushes, and soap
Camp stove and propane
Blankets or sleeping bags
First aid kit
Flashlight and batteries
Money (bills and small change)
Pet food, if you have a pet
Out-of-state contact telephone number
Paper plates, cups
Potty seat, bags, and tissue
Extra socks and underwear

Builder-Upper:
I Am Powerful!

Bingzy says, "Reading makes me powerful and determined to do my best."

I Am Powerful: I am determined and use willpower.

Read the questions and discuss.

1. How does learning to do things by yourself make you powerful?
2. How does being determined help you learn something new?
3. How do you show you are determined to take care of the environment?
4. How can willpower help you do the right thing when someone wants you to do something wrong?
5. Are you determined to learn the lessons taught in the Builder-Uppers? Name the Builder-Uppers you have learned.
6. When have you been determined to do your best?

Name: ______________________________

Builder-Upper:
I Am Powerful!

Bingzy says, "I am powerful when I become more independent."

ACTIVITY

Put an X in the box next to the things you do by yourself.

- ☐ I tie my shoes.
- ☐ I comb my hair.
- ☐ I keep my face and hands clean.
- ☐ I help prepare my lunch.
- ☐ I get my school clothes ready the night before.
- ☐ I brush my teeth twice a day.
- ☐ I pick up my toys.
- ☐ I make my bed.

READ & DISCUSS

Which activities do not have an X? Why? Work with someone to help you with these.

Can you think of two more things you do that make you powerful?

Discuss them with other family members.

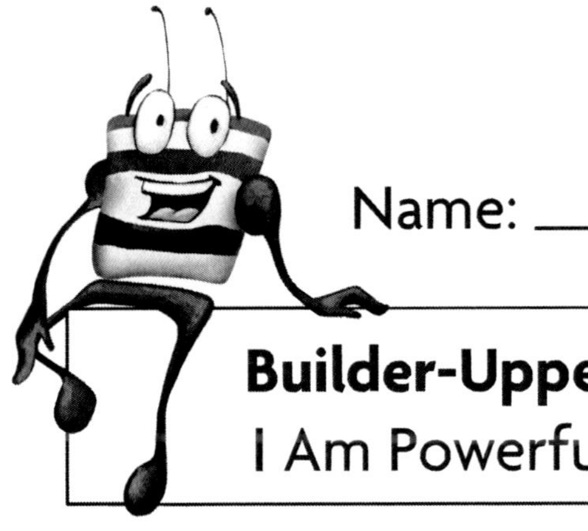

Name: ______________________________

Builder-Upper:
I Am Powerful!

Bingzy says, "Reading books makes for powerful learning."

Read aloud and discuss.

Bingzy says, "Come read with me.
I have a book for you.
Sharing stories with your friends
Is a cool, cool thing to do."

Through reading you gain knowledge.
That is powerful, indeed.
Learning comes from reading books,
So pick up a book and read!

ACTIVITY

1. **Count how many books you can find in the picture.**

   Write the number here ____________.

2. **Read your favorite book to someone. Tell them why it's your favorite book.**

Name: ______________________________

Builder-Upper:
I Am Powerful!

Bingzy says, "Learning the Builder-Uppers makes me powerful."

ACTIVITY

Read aloud and discuss. Circle the Builder-Uppers in the word search.

I AM **STRONG** AND **POWERFUL**, **HEALTHY** AND **LOVING**, **HARMONIOUS** AND **CREATIVE**, **SUCCESSFUL** AND **HAPPY**.

H	A	R	M	O	N	I	O	U	S
A	O	L	O	V	I	N	G	E	T
P	B	F	D	J	K	X	Z	I	R
P	H	E	A	L	T	H	Y	M	O
Y	P	O	W	E	R	F	U	L	N
C	R	E	A	T	I	V	E	Q	G
S	U	C	C	E	S	S	F	U	L

Name: ______________________________

Builder-Upper:
I Am Powerful!

Bingzy says, "When you listen to others, you can learn something new."

Read the story aloud and discuss.

Joey wanted to make the soccer team. He asked his father what he should do.

"You need to be healthy and in good shape to play soccer, or any other sport," Dad said. "Let's make a list of things that will help you."

1. Eat healthy meals.
2. Limit your sugary/salty treats.
3. Drink lots of water every day.
4. Get more exercise and spend less time watching TV.
5. Learn the rules of the game and practice.

"I can do that," Joey said.

"Good. I'll help you. Get the ball and we'll go to the park and start kicking it around!"

Joey gave a thumbs up. "Thanks, Dad," he smiled. "You rock!"

READ & DISCUSS

Was Joey smart to discuss his problem with his dad? Why?

What new things did Joey learn from his dad?

What new things have you learned today?

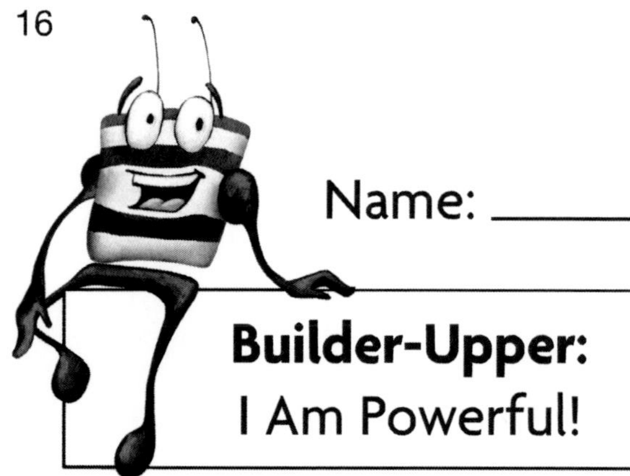

Name: ______________________________

Builder-Upper:
I Am Powerful!

Bingzy says, "Growing food is a powerful learning experience."

Read aloud and discuss.

Bingzy is proud of his garden. He planted tomatoes this year. He says they are easy to grow in the ground or in a pot, as long as they have good soil, sunlight, and water.

When you buy a tomato plant or seeds, you'll learn some of their names, like Better Boy, Creole, Big Boy, and Early Girl.

Tomatoes are used in some of our favorite meals: spaghetti, meatloaf, and chili. They are sensational in salsa too. How about a bacon, lettuce, and tomato sandwich? Yummy!

ACTIVITY

Color the tomatoes on Bingzy's seed packet.

Maybe you can grow your own tomatoes and other vegetables. It's a healthy and fun thing to do!

What other foods would you like to grow?

Name: ____________________

Builder-Upper:
I Am Powerful!

Bingzy says, "I am powerful when I learn to recognize shapes."

Read aloud and discuss.

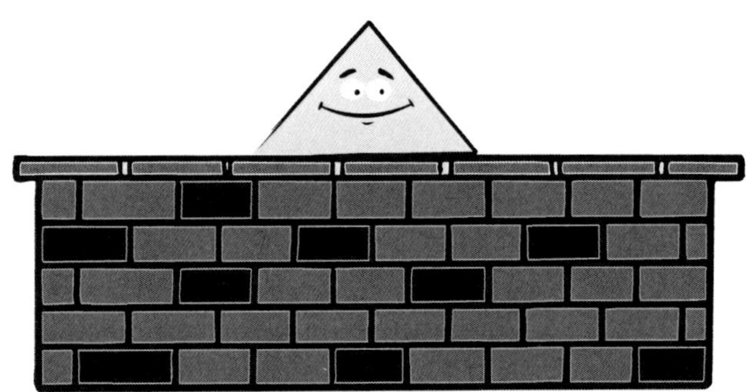

Triangle sat on a rectangle wall.
Ouch, he got hit by a bouncing ball.
The bouncing ball knocked him off the wall,
Hitting a circle with no sides at all.

ACTIVITY

Draw a picture to show what you recall.

1. **Who got knocked off the wall?**
2. **Who has no sides at all?**
3. **What was the shape of the wall?**

Trace and color the square. A square has four sides. All of the sides are the same.

Builder-Upper:
I Am Healthy!

Bingzy says, "Name some things you can do to stay healthy."

I Am Healthy: I take good care of my body.

Read the questions and discuss.

1. What does it mean to be healthy?
2. What are your favorite fruits and vegetables? Which ones did you eat today?
3. What are your favorite fruit juices?
4. Why should you brush your teeth at least twice a day? When should you brush your teeth?
5. What are some good ways to exercise your body?
6. How can you be safe around water?

Name: ______________________________

Builder-Upper:
I Am Healthy!

Bingzy says, "Fruits and vegetables keep you healthy."

Read aloud and discuss.

Apples, oranges, and bananas;
Grapes, peaches, and pears;
Cherries and all kinds of berries–
There's delicious fruit everywhere.

Corn, squash, and zucchini;
Potatoes, beans, and peas;
Cabbage, kale, and carrots–
Pass the vegetable soup, please.

READ & DISCUSS

What fruit would you put in your fruit salad?

What vegetables would you put in your soup?

Name and color the fruits and vegetables in the picture.

Name: ______________________________

Builder-Upper:
I Am Healthy!

Bingzy says, "Fruit juices are healthy drinks."

ACTIVITY

Read aloud and discuss. Do you like fruit juices?
They are good for most people. Fruit juices come in many colors and flavors.
Draw a line to match the type of juice and its color.

YELLOW	BLUEBERRY
PURPLE	TOMATO
RED	LEMONADE
ORANGE	GRAPE
BLUE	ORANGE

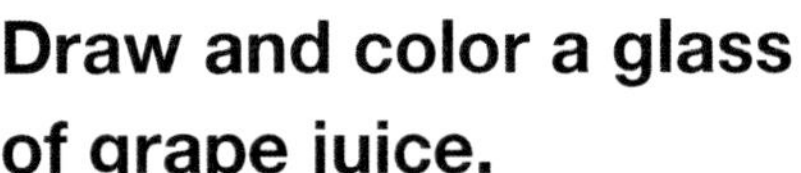

Draw and color a glass of grape juice.

Draw and color a can of tomato juice.

Draw and color a pitcher of orange juice.

Name: ____________________

Builder-Upper:
I Am Healthy!

Bingzy says, "I eat food from each of the food groups."

ACTIVITY

Read and discuss the food group pyramid.

What would you like to eat today?

Surprise your mom or dad and ask if you can plan today's menu.

Be sure to choose food from each food group.

FATS

GRAINS VEGGIES FRUIT DAIRY MEATS & BEANS

1. Breakfast

____

____

____

2. Lunch

____

____

3. Dinner

____

____

____

4. Snack

____

____

Name: ____________________

Builder-Upper:
I Am Healthy!

Bingzy says, "Brush, brush, brush your teeth. Brush the germs away. Then give a smile to everyone. It's the Bingzy way!"

READ & DISCUSS

How often do you visit the dentist?

How often do you brush your teeth?

Do you brush your teeth without complaining?

Good for you!

ACTIVITY

Draw a picture of your family members and their happy smiles.

Name: ______________________________

Builder-Upper:
I Am Healthy!

Bingzy says, "Drinking water is good for you."

READ & DISCUSS

Bingzy has some good advice.
He may have to say it twice.
Drink plenty of water every day.
It helps to keep the doctor away!

When you run and exercise,
Drinking water is really wise.
It will boost your energy.
It's what you need, I guarantee.

Watermelon and cucumbers have a high percentage of water.

What other things can you eat or drink that will give your body water?

If you don't know any, ask your teacher or parents for ideas.

What exercises do you do?

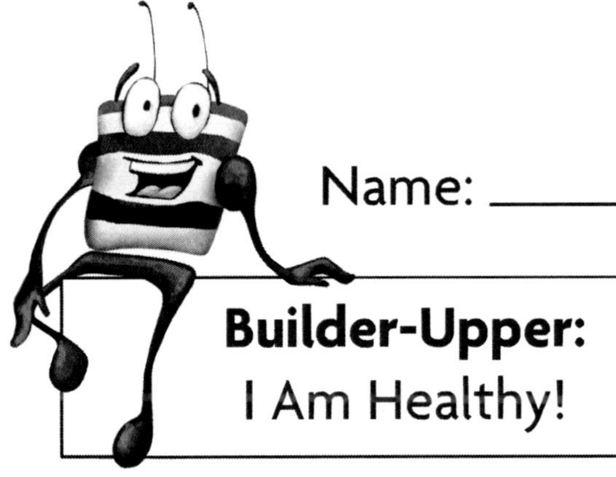

Name: ____________________

Builder-Upper:
I Am Healthy!

Bingzy says, "Keeping your body clean helps to keep you healthy."

READ & DISCUSS

Always be "water smart" in a pool or tub.

Talk to your parents about water safety rules.

Read aloud and discuss.

Bath time is a good time with Bingzy.

Jump in, yellow ducky.
The water is just right.
Not too hot, not too cold
For a bubble bath tonight!

ACTIVITY

Where should you put soap when it is not being used? Why?

Look at the picture. Name three things Bingzy should do when he finishes his bath.

Builder-Upper:
I Am Loving!

Bingzy says, "Encouraging words make us more loving."

I Am Loving: I care about others.

Read the questions and discuss.

1. What does it mean to be loving?
2. Who loves you? Who do you love?
3. Can hugs and smiles be expressions of love? Why?
4. How can you show your love to animals?
5. What words are loving words? Did you use any today?
6. What did someone say to encourage you or make you feel good today?

Name: ____________________

Builder-Upper:
I Am Loving!

Bingzy says, "Be kind and considerate of others."

Read aloud and discuss.

It is important to be kind and considerate to the members of your family. Here are some suggestions. **Can you think of other ways to show that you are becoming a more loving person?**

ACTIVITY

Things you can do for your parents:

1. Give a hug and say, "I love you."
2. Pick up your toys without being asked.
3. Go to bed without complaining.
4. Help take out the trash.
5. Put your dirty clothes in the clothes hamper.

Things you can do for your brothers or sisters:

1. Share your toys.
2. Always ask permission to use their stuff.
3. Try to avoid arguing with family members.

Things you can do for your grandma and grandpa:

1. Draw a picture for them.
2. Sing a song in person or over the phone.
3. Offer to help rake leaves or do some other job for them.

Name: ______________________________

Builder-Upper:
I Am Loving!

Bingzy says, "Spend time with grandparents."

Read aloud and discuss.

My granny is so nice to me.
I love to sit upon her knee.
She tells me about days gone by,
And often sings a lullaby.

As Granny rocks me to and fro,
She tells me things I need to know.
When we're together it's so much fun,
Saying Builder-Uppers one by one.

I am Strong and Powerful,
Healthy and Loving,
Harmonious and Creative,
Successful and Happy.

Saying the Builder-Uppers reminds
Bingzy to believe in himself.

READ & DISCUSS

Do you need to be reminded too?

Can you think of ways that you have been a loving person?

How many Builder-Uppers can you recite?

Name: ______________________________

Builder-Upper:
I Am Loving!

Bingzy says, "Smile to brighten someone's day."

Read aloud and discuss.

A new girl was introduced to our class. She looked scared because she didn't know anyone. I gave her a big smile hoping to make her feel better. It worked! When it was time for recess, she seemed happy when I stood next to her and we walked out together.

READ & DISCUSS

What can you do to help a new student in your classroom?

What are some important school rules everyone follows?

What game can you teach a new student to play?

Name: ______________________________

Builder-Upper:
I Am Loving!

Bingzy says, "Give special gifts from your heart."

ACTIVITY

Color the flowers in the vase.

Color the frame too.

Give your picture to someone special, as a gift from you!

Name: ______________________________

Builder-Upper:
I Am Loving!

Bingzy says, "Be kind to animals."

Read aloud and discuss.

One day when Bingzy was watering tomato plants in his backyard, he heard a whimpering noise. He listened closely and heard a cry coming from the other side of his garden wall. "Maybe something is wrong at neighbor Bill's house," he thought. Bingzy flew to the top of the wall and looked over. No one was home except for Bill's new puppy, Petie.

"What's the matter Petie-boy?" Bingzy called as he flew down to the puppy. Bingzy saw that Petie had knocked over his water bowl and didn't have any water. His tongue was hanging out and he was panting hard.

"Poor puppy," Bingzy said. "I'll get you some water." Bingzy filled the water bowl, petted Petie, and then flew back home.

"Thank you, Bingzy," Petie barked.

READ & DISCUSS

Wasn't that a loving thing for Bingzy to do?

Have you helped anyone lately?

Are you kind to animals?

What kind of pet would you like?

How would you take care of it?

Name: ______________________________

Builder-Upper:
I Am Loving!

Bingzy says, "Listen to others and try to help them solve problems."

LETTERS TO BINGZY

Dear Bingzy,

My mother makes me play with her friend's son, Todd, when he comes to visit. He takes my toys without asking and leaves them for me to pick up. He doesn't know how to pitch or catch the ball. My mother gets mad at me if I have trouble with Todd. He is five years old and I am seven. What should I do?

Angry Mike

Dear Mike,

Don't be angry. Todd is a lot younger than you. It sounds as if he needs to learn how to be a good visitor in your home. Since you are older, why don't you talk to him and explain that you have rules in your house. If he's to be your friend, he will need to learn the rules. Maybe your rules could be something like this:

1. **Always ask before playing with someone else's toys.**
2. **Always put the toys away after playing with them.**

If he doesn't know how to play with a ball, maybe he hasn't had a chance to learn. Why don't you teach him? You could also teach him how a loving person treats someone. That loving person is YOU! You can, you can, you can!

Love,
Bingzy

READ & DISCUSS

What did Bingzy suggest Mike should do?

Do you have any other suggestions for Mike?

Builder-Upper:
I Am Harmonious!

Bingzy says, "Harmonious people are fun to be with."

I Am Harmonious: I get along with others.

Read the questions and discuss.

1. What does it mean to be harmonious? How can you tell when you have made someone happy, or when you have hurt their feelings?

2. How can your family be harmonious when you watch television?

3. What are some polite words that harmonious people use?

4. How are you harmonious with others who are different from you?

5. How can you help your classroom be harmonious?

6. How do you include other kids at playtime?

Name: ______________________________

Builder-Upper:
I Am Harmonious!

Bingzy says, "Reading faces tells us how others feel."

ACTIVITY

Can you tell by looking at someone's face if he or she is happy?

This is called "reading faces." Play a game with friends and see if anyone can guess the emotion you are showing. Choose from the list below or add your own.

HAPPY	**SCARED**	**SORRY**	**SURPRISED**
SICK	**EXCITED**	**TIRED**	**SAD**

Can you "read" Bingzy's faces below?

Name: ______________________________

Builder-Upper:
I Am Harmonious!

Bingzy says, "Be harmonious! Try getting along with family members."

Read aloud and discuss.

Samantha was quietly playing with her doll family. She was changing the baby's dress when her older brother, Andrew, snatched the doll from her. He dangled it in the air and held it too high for Samantha to reach.

ACTIVITY **Choose the best ending to this story.**

A Samantha started crying and ran to Mother to tell what Andrew had done. Mother scolded him and made him give the doll back. Samantha stopped crying and smiled. She was glad that Andrew got in trouble.

Andrew was mad. He said, "You didn't have to tell on me. I was just playing."

Discuss how Samantha felt. How did Andrew feel?
Draw a mouth to show how Samantha felt.
Draw a mouth to show how Andrew felt.

B Samantha said, "Stop, Andrew. Give it back to me."

Andrew said, "Not until you say you'll play with me."

Samantha said, "Well, okay. But let me finish dressing my doll. Do you want to play Go Fish?"

Discuss how Samantha felt. How did Andrew feel?
Which ending was better? Why?
Have you had to solve a similar problem?
How did you solve your problem?

Name: ________________________________

Builder-Upper:
I Am Harmonious!

Bingzy says, "Always use polite words."

ACTIVITY

We want to be thoughtful of others. That's why we say words that are respectful and kind. Act out situations with your family or friends to decide when and how you could use the following polite phrases and sentences.

Use polite words every day.

How does it feel to be polite?

Do you know someone who needs to learn these words?

Could you teach them, politely?

May I?

Excuse me.

I'm sorry.

You're welcome.

Thank you.

No, thank you.

Pass the bread, please.

May I please have the remote control?

Is this seat taken?

May I please have a glass of water?

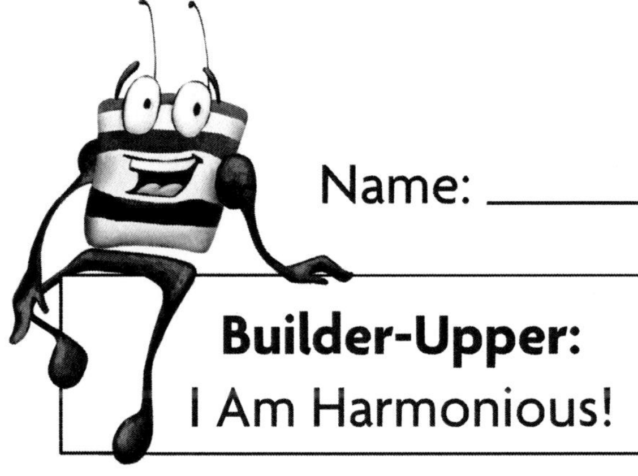

Name: ______________________________

Builder-Upper:
I Am Harmonious!

Bingzy says, "Friends look different but are the same on the inside."

My Friends

Tiffany's skin is brown.
Joshua's eyes are blue.
Berto's hair is black,
And Maria's is too.

LaMar wears glasses.
Rhoda's in a chair with wheels.
Sean is a diabetic
And has to have special meals.

Tammy wears a hearing aid.
Annie is autistic.
Kelly likes to draw and paint.
We say she is artistic.

Tyrone is very smart
And gets the answers first.
Jasmine always wants to talk
Or she thinks she's gonna burst.

Ronny and Donny are twins
And we can't tell who is who.
They are the same but different
Just like me and you.

The things that make us different
Right from the start
Can soon be forgotten
When we look with just our heart.

ACTIVITY

Circle the words below which describe a friend when you look at them with just your heart.

SELFISH HELPFUL HONEST
UNFAIR LOVING MEAN KIND

Select and give examples of one of the words you have circled.

____
____
____
____
____
____
____
____
____
____
____

Name: ______________________________

Builder-Upper:
I Am Harmonious!

Bingzy says, "It is fun to display pictures of family and friends."

ACTIVITY

Make a mobile of your friends!

You can make a mobile to remind you of your friends. All you will need is a clothes hanger, yarn, scissors, a hole punch, and photographs of your friends. The drawing will show you how to put your mobile together. When it is finished, you can hang it in your favorite place. Have fun!

Step 1: Take pictures of your friends. If you want, cut the pictures into funny shapes!

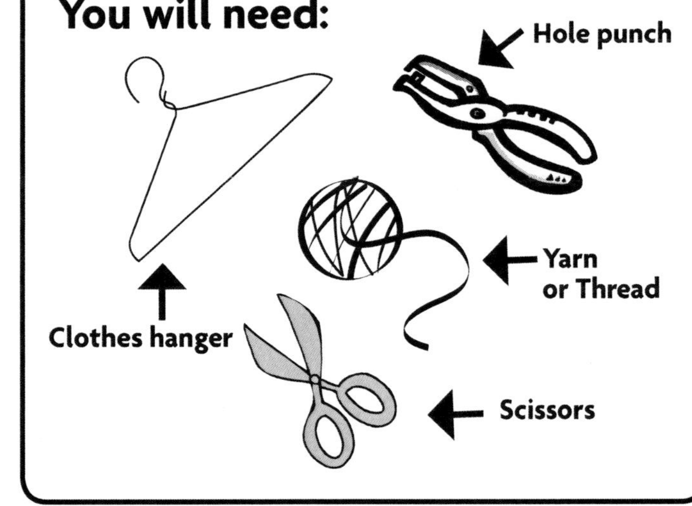

Step 2: Use the hole punch to punch holes in the top of the pictures.

Step 3: Take a piece of yarn and put it through the hole in the photo. Tie a bow. If you don't know how to tie a bow, ask an adult for help.

Step 4: Take each picture and tie it to the clothes hanger.

Ta-da! Now you have a picture mobile!

Name: ______________________________

Builder-Upper:
I Am Harmonious!

Bingzy says, "Being part of a group makes me harmonious."

The children on the playground were having lots of fun.
They were jumping and laughing, all except one.
Elly stood off by herself; she was sad and shy.
She wanted to join the others, but she didn't even try.

No one noticed Elly, except Tommy Clay.
He went over to her and said, "Come on, Elly. Let's play."
It made her feel much better to be invited by name.
She was happier after that and always played the game.

READ & DISCUSS

Do you know someone who is shy?

How do you think it feels to be shy?

What can you do to make a shy person feel more comfortable?

Builder-Upper:
I Am Creative!

Bingzy says, "You can be creative through dance, music, art, and words."

I Am Creative: I use my imagination to come up with things.

Read the questions and discuss.

1. Do you like to be creative? Why?
2. What have you created with recyclables? How else can you help to improve the environment?
3. What is your favorite way to be creative?
4. Where is your favorite place to be creative?
5. How can you be creative when you dance to Bingzy's songs?
6. How do music, pictures, and nature help you be creative?

Name: ______________________________

Builder-Upper:
I Am Creative!

Bingzy says, "Look up, down, and all around for creative things you can see."

ACTIVITY

Read the story aloud and draw a picture of what Bingzy sees.

Bingzy likes to learn
From every sight and sound.
He looks up into the blue, blue sky
While lying on the ground.

He sees a sheep made out of clouds.
He sees a bird go by.
He sees the trees above his head.
He sees an airplane fly.

"Looking up is good," Bingzy says,
"As well as looking down.
There is much to see in our big world,
So look up, down, and all around."

Name: ______________________________

Builder-Upper:
I Am Creative!

Bingzy says, "Be creative. Find another use for plastic water bottles."

READ & DISCUSS

When we use things again and again, we call it "recycling." Bingzy and his friends are at the recycling center.

What are they recycling?

What things do you throw away that could be used again?

Be creative and think of other items that you could reuse. Make a list of these items. Add to the list regularly.

Name: ______________________________

Builder-Upper:
I Am Creative!

Bingzy says, "Draw pictures of my friends."

ACTIVITY

Read aloud and discuss.

Bingzy has friends in all sizes, shapes, and colors.
Here are some of his friends.

See if you can draw them. What names would you give Bingzy's friends? Can you draw a new friend for Bingzy?
Now, draw yourself with Bingzy's new friend.

Name: ____________________

Builder-Upper:
I Am Creative!

Bingzy says, "Experiment with colors."

Read aloud and discuss.

It was a rainy day and there were puddles everywhere. Bingzy had on his rain boots to keep his feet dry, and an umbrella to keep him from getting wet. As Bingzy walked along, he looked up in the sky and saw a beautiful rainbow. He saw red, orange, yellow, green, blue, indigo, and violet. Bingzy decided to choose three of the colors to make his own rainbow.

ACTIVITY

Color the picture and make a rainbow in the sky.

Name: ______________________________

Builder-Upper:
I Am Creative!

Bingzy says, "Draw some pretty flowers."

ACTIVITY

You can learn to draw pretty flowers. Look at the ones on this page. Some are not finished. Complete the pattern to make the flowers. Now draw a flower all by yourself.

Remember, the more you draw, the better you will get. So, have fun!

Name: ______________________________

Builder-Upper:
I Am Creative!

Bingzy says, "Be creative and make a stick puppet."

Here's Bingzy!

ACTIVITY

You can have your own Bingzy: Just color him and cut him out.

If you want to make him into a puppet, glue him to an art stick, or punch a hole near the top of the paper and tie it on a string.
(Ask for help if you need it!)

Have fun!

Builder-Upper:
I Am Successful!

Bingzy says, "To be a success, you should always do your best."

I Am Successful: I finish what I start.

Read the questions and discuss.

1. What does it mean to be successful when doing your homework? What household chores do you successfully complete?
2. How can you be successful in the classroom?
3. How does it make you feel to be successful?
4. Why should you feel successful when you are organized?
5. Why is it important to always do your best?
6. Have you completed your work today?

Name: ____________________

Builder-Upper:
I Am Successful!

Bingzy says, "I am successful when I reach my goal of counting to 20."

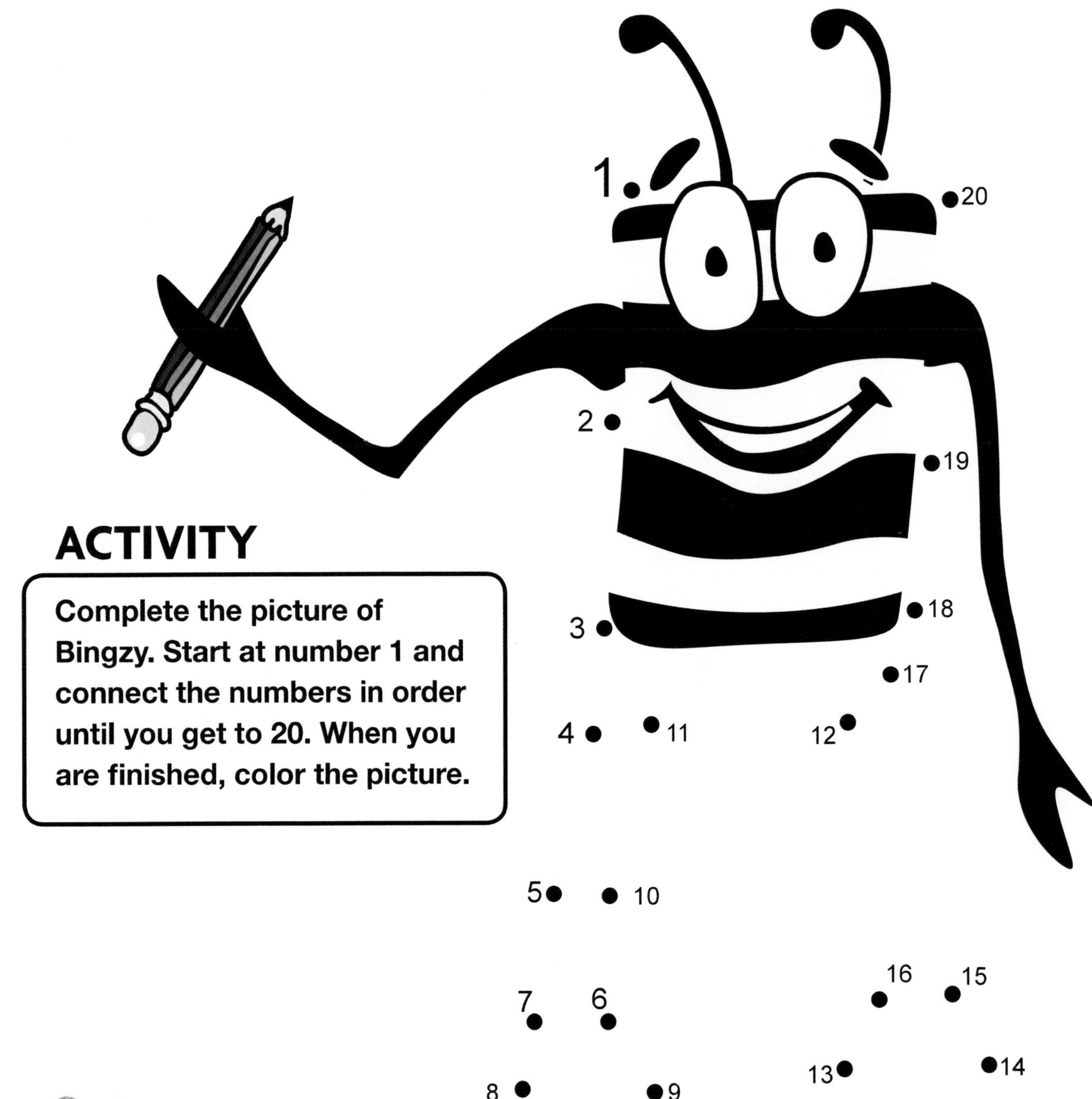

ACTIVITY

Complete the picture of Bingzy. Start at number 1 and connect the numbers in order until you get to 20. When you are finished, color the picture.

Name: ______________________________

Builder-Upper:
I Am Successful!

Bingzy says, "I am successful when I work hard to solve word puzzles."

ACROSS

DOWN

1.

3.

4.

2.

5.

ACTIVITY

HAPPY	**HARMONIOUS**	**LOVING**
CREATIVE	**HEALTHY**	**BINGZY**

ACROSS

1. Eating fruits and veggies keeps me __________.
4. I give gifts from my heart. I am ______________.
5. When I experiment with colors I am __________.

DOWN

1. I laugh and I have fun. I am _____________.
2. I get along with others. I am _____________.
3. Who says to believe in yourself?____________.

Name: ___________________________________

Builder-Upper:
I Am Successful!

Bingzy says, "Help me find my lost balloons!"

ACTIVITY

After you find the balloons, color the picture.

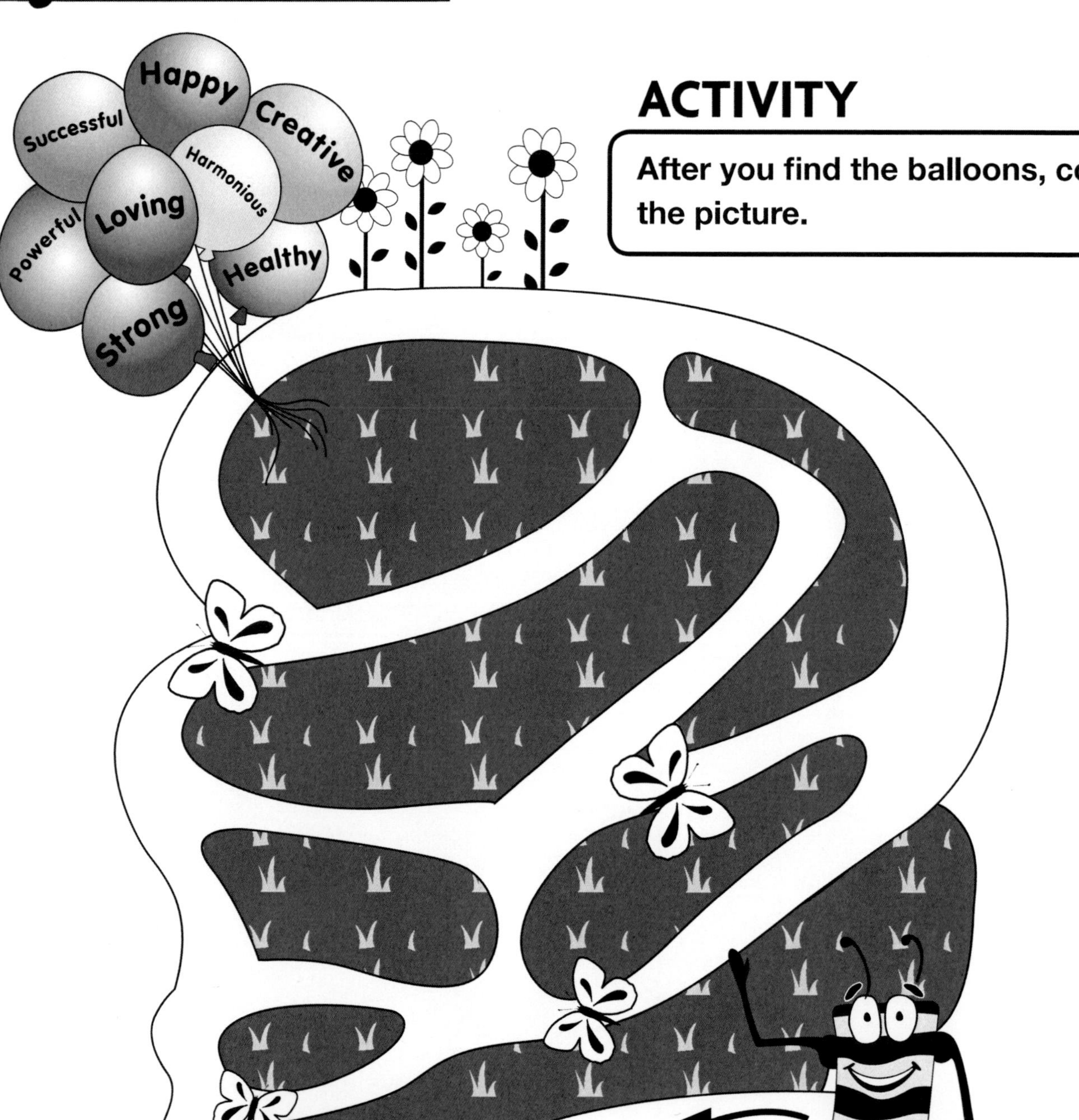

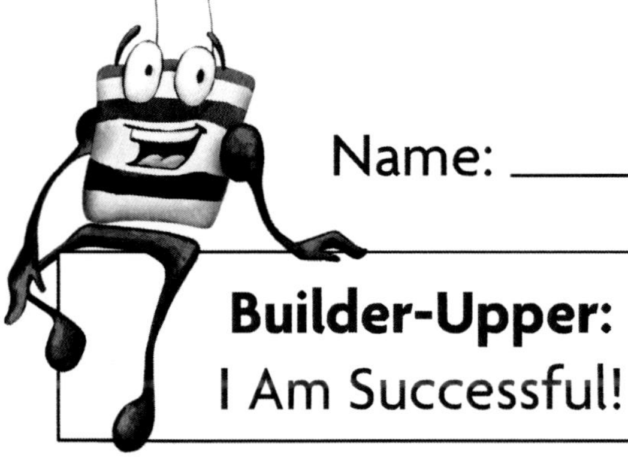

Name: ____________________

Builder-Upper:
I Am Successful!

Bingzy says, "I am successful when I start my day by being organized."

READ & DISCUSS

Read aloud and discuss.

Josh and Bingzy were in a hurry to get to school. "Why are you looking so sad, Josh?" Bingzy asked.

Josh replied, "Because I have trouble getting to school on time. I'm always running late, can't find my homework, and don't know what I'm going to wear. Man, I hate getting up early!"

Bingzy patted Josh on the back. "Hey buddy, do what I do! I help Mom make my lunch the night before, and as soon as I do my homework, I put it in my backpack and leave it by the door. I put all my clothes out the night before too, and then I'm ready to hop in them in the morning. It's a cinch!"

"That sounds like a good idea, Bingzy," Josh said with a smile. "I'll try it."

Bingzy added, "I even set the table for breakfast with my cereal bowl, spoon, and box of cereal."

Josh giggled. "But not the milk!"

"No!" Bingzy laughed. "Not the milk!"

How about you? Could you make your mornings more successful by being ready and set to go?

Discuss the proper bedtime hour.

Discuss the appropriate time and place to do homework.

Discuss ways you can make morning activities successful.

Name: ______________________________

Builder-Upper:
I Am Successful!

Bingzy says, "I am successful when I find the names of the missing Builder-Uppers."

ACTIVITY

Write the missing Builder-Uppers on the balloons. HINT: They begin with the letter "H" and end with the letter "Y."

Color the balloons.

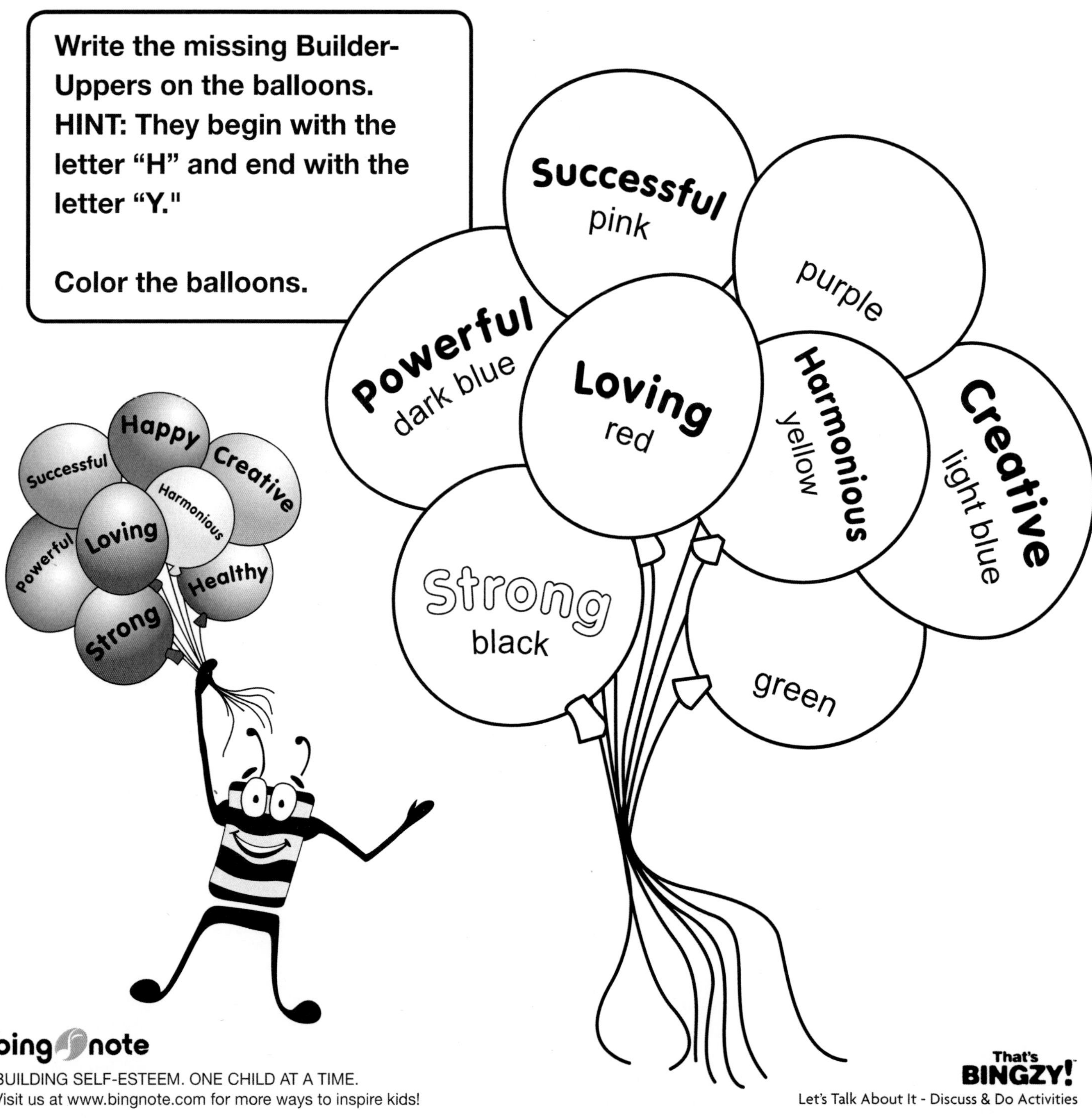

Name: ______________________________

Builder-Upper:
I Am Successful!

Bingzy says, "Puzzles are fun and they help us learn."

ACTIVITY

Color the picture. Glue it to heavier paper and let it dry. Cut on the dotted lines and then put it back together again! (Maybe you would like to share it with a friend.)

Builder-Upper: I Am Happy!

Bingzy says, "I like being around happy people."

I Am Happy: I feel good.

Read the questions and discuss.

1. Do you have a special place that makes you happy?
2. Why do we have Happy Birthday cards?
3. What things do you do to make others happy?
4. What is something someone did to make you happy?
5. What songs do you sing that make you happy?
6. How can you tell when someone is happy?

Name: ______________________________

Builder-Upper:
I Am Happy!

Bingzy says, "Find your own special place."

Read aloud and discuss.

I have a very special place:
The swing in my backyard.
It's always waiting there for me,
Hanging from my big oak tree.

When I'm angry or upset,
My swing seems to say to me,
"Come my friend and swing awhile.
Flying fast, I'll make you smile."

Up, up I go into the sky,
Swinging high and swinging low.
Soon all my anger flies away,
And happy thoughts swing my way.

READ & DISCUSS

When you get angry or upset, where is your special place?

Who do you share your problems with?

Who is the best problem-solver in your house?

Name: ______________________________

Builder-Upper:
I Am Happy!

Bingzy says, "Giving gifts from the heart makes me happy!"

READ & DISCUSS

What gifts have you received that did not cost money?
What can you make and give as a gift?
How does it make you feel to give gifts?

Name: ______________________

Builder-Upper:
I Am Happy!

Bingzy says, "Helping others is a good thing to do and will make you happy."

READ & DISCUSS

Bingzy saw his elderly neighbor working in the yard. He asked, "May I help you, Mrs. Brown? I can put the leaves in bags and take them to the trash cans."

She answered, "Why thank you, Bingzy. What a good friend you are!"

Bingzy sang a cheerful song as he buzzed around the yard. It made him happy to be helpful.

When the cans were full and the yard was nice and clean, Mrs. Brown said, "How about a glass of lemonade and a cookie made with honey?"

"That sounds great!" Bingzy said with a smile.

Can you remember when you helped someone?
How did it make you feel? Name some ways you can help others.
How do you feel when you do something without being asked? Why?

Name: ____________________

Builder-Upper:
I Am Happy!

Bingzy says, "Playing with friends of all ages makes me happy."

ACTIVITY

Read aloud and discuss.

Adam is eight years old.
Roberto is one year old.
Jack is two years old.
Hannah is nine years old.
Clark is seven years old.
Patrick is four years old.
Anna is five years old.
Ethan is three years old.
Madison is ten years old.

Who is the oldest?

____

Who is the youngest?

____

How many boys are listed?

____

How many girls are listed?

____

10
9
8
7
6
5
4
3
2
1

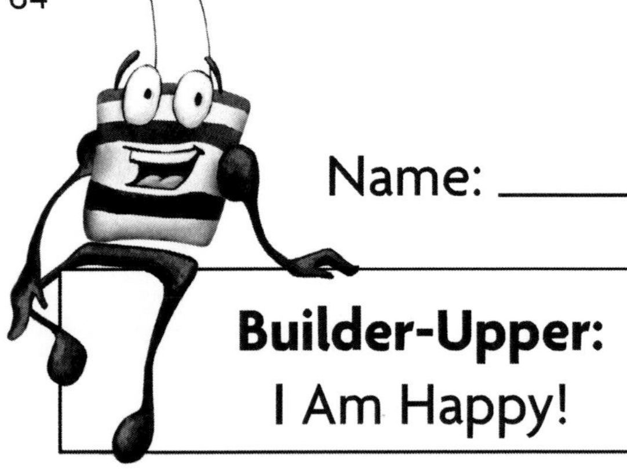

Name: ______________________________

Builder-Upper:
I Am Happy!

Bingzy says, "I sing and dance to happy songs."

Read aloud and discuss.

I clap my hands to a happy song.
I like to sing, so I sing along.
I move my feet to a snappy beat
And share my joy with those I meet.

Music can be fun and exciting too.
You can hop around like a kangaroo,
Flap your wings like a bird in the sky,
Or act like a soldier marching by.

READ & DISCUSS

Listen to one of your favorite songs.

What are the words telling you?

Does the music have a snappy beat?

Does the music make you want to march or hop around?

Is it a song you want to share with others? Why?

Name: ______________________________

Builder-Upper:
I Am Happy!

Bingzy says, "Getting good grades makes me happy. I counted the chicks and received a happy face."

READ & DISCUSS

Read aloud and discuss.

Momma Hen had baby chicks.
They needed a lot of care.
Whenever she tried to count them all,
They scattered everywhere.

The chicks were a colorful sight.
Two speckled chicks were black and white.
Four had feathers that were pretty and brown.
One white chick just sat right down
While three yellow chicks paraded around.

ACTIVITY

Color and count the chicks and you can get a happy face too.

How many chicks does Momma Hen have?

Color one chick white.

Color two chicks black and white.

Color four chicks brown.

Color three chicks yellow.

Stay on this road with me.
Together, we're a team.
We have a goal, you see:
It's building SELF-ESTEEM!

Please don't let this be the end.
Travel with me again.
Building up kids' self-esteem
Brings happiness deep within.